The Wedding [...] om Handle and Who Was in It

# The Wedding Procession of the Rag Doll and the Broom Handle and Who Was in It

by Carl Sandburg            Pictures by Harriet Pincus

Harcourt Brace Jovanovich, Publishers

San Diego   New York   London

*also by Carl Sandburg*
ABE LINCOLN GROWS UP
EARLY MOON
PRAIRIE-TOWN BOY
ROOTABAGA STORIES
THE SANDBURG TREASURY
WIND SONG
*edited by Lee Bennett Hopkins*
RAINBOWS ARE MADE: Poems by Carl Sandburg

Printed in the United States of America

Library of Congress Cataloging in Publication Data

Sandburg, Carl, 1878–1967.
The wedding procession of the rag doll and the
broom handle and who was in it.

SUMMARY: The rag doll and the broom handle marry
and have a grand wedding procession that includes
the Easy Ticklers, the Chubby Chubbs, and the
Sleepyheads.
[1. Weddings–Fiction] I. Pincus, Harriet. II. Title.
[PZ7.S1965We  1978]    [E]    78-7912
ISBN 0-15-294930-5   ISBN 0-15-695487-7 (pbk.)
J K L M N O       B C D E F G

The Rag Doll had many friends. The Whisk Broom, the Furnace Shovel, the Coffee Pot, they all liked the Rag Doll very much.

But when the Rag Doll married, it was the Broom Handle she picked because the Broom Handle fixed her eyes.

A proud child, proud but careless, banged the head of the Rag Doll against a door one day and knocked off both the glass eyes sewed on long ago. It was then the Broom Handle found two black California prunes and fastened the two

California prunes just where the eyes belonged. So then the Rag Doll had two fine black eyes brand new. She was even nicknamed Black Eyes by some people.

There was a wedding when the Rag Doll married the Broom Handle. It was a grand wedding with one of the grandest processions ever seen at a rag doll wedding. And we are sure no broom handle ever had a grander wedding procession when he got married.

Who marched in the procession? Well, first came the Spoon Lickers. Every one of them had a teaspoon, or a soupspoon, though most of them had a big tablespoon. On the spoons, what did they have? Oh, some had butterscotch,

some had gravy, some had marshmallow fudge. Every one had something slickery sweet or fat to eat on the spoon. And as they marched in the wedding procession of the Rag Doll and the Broom Handle, they licked their spoons and looked around and licked their spoons again.

Next came the Tin Pan Bangers. Some had dishpans, some had frying pans, some had potato peeling pans. All the pans were tin with tight tin bottoms. And the Tin Pan Bangers banged with knives and forks and iron and wooden

bangers on the bottoms of the tin pans. And as they marched in the wedding procession of the Rag Doll and the Broom Handle, they banged their pans and looked around and banged again.

Then came the Chocolate Chins. They were all eating chocolates. And the chocolate was slippery and slickered all over their chins. Some of them spattered the ends of their noses with black chocolate. Some of them spread the

brown chocolate nearly up to their ears. And then as they marched in the wedding procession of the Rag Doll and the Broom Handle, they stuck their chins in the air and looked around and stuck their chins in the air again.

Then came the Dirty Bibs. They wore plain white bibs, checker bibs, stripe bibs, blue bibs, and bibs with butterflies. But all the bibs were dirty. The plain white bibs were dirty, the checker bibs were dirty, the stripe bibs, the blue

bibs, and the bibs with butterflies on them, they were all dirty. And so in the wedding procession of the Rag Doll and the Broom Handle, the Dirty Bibs marched with their dirty fingers on the bibs, and they looked around and laughed and looked around and laughed again.

Next came the Clean Ears. They were proud. How they got into the procession nobody knows. Their ears were all clean. They were clean not only on the outside, but they were clean on the inside. There was not a speck of dirt

or dust or muss or mess on the inside nor the outside of their ears. And so in the wedding procession of the Rag Doll and the Broom Handle, they wiggled their ears and looked around and wiggled their ears again.

The Easy Ticklers were next in the procession. Their faces were shining. Their cheeks were like bars of new soap. Their ribs were strong, and the meat and the fat was thick on their ribs. It was plain to see they were saying,

"Don't tickle me because I tickle so easy." And as they marched in the wedding procession of the Rag Doll and the Broom Handle, they tickled themselves and laughed and looked around and tickled themselves again.

The music was furnished mostly by the Musical Soup Eaters. They marched with big bowls of soup in front of them and big spoons for eating the soup. They whistled and chuzzled and snozzled the soup, and the noise they made

could be heard far up at the head of the procession where the Spoon Lickers were marching. So they dipped their soup and looked around and dipped their soup again.

The Chubby Chubs were next. They were roly-poly, round-faced smackers and snoozers. They were not fat babies—oh no, oh no—not fat but just chubby

and easy to squeeze. They marched on their chubby legs and chubby feet and chubbed their chubbs and looked around and chubbed their chubbs again.

The last of all in the wedding procession of the Rag Doll and the Broom Handle were the Sleepyheads. They were smiling and glad to be marching, but their heads were slimpsing down and their smiles were half fading away

and their eyes were half shut or a little more than half shut. They staggered just a little as though their feet were not sure where they were going. They were the Sleepyheads, the last of all in the wedding procession of the Rag Doll and the Broom Handle, and the Sleepyheads, they never looked around at all.

It *was* a grand procession, don't you think so?